Montserrat

Text: Esteve Serra i Pérez
Layout: Eduard Busquets
Photographs: A. Guillén, J. Oliva, S. Gómez, E. Valero,
P. Fernández, E. Busquets
Thanks to: Abadia de Montserrat,
Agrícola Regional, S.A., Jordi Cuesta and
Patronat de la Muntanya de Montserrat

Edition revised 2016

Dip.Legal: B-17726-2014
© C.I.F. A08187056

To you, who visit Montserrat

Saint Mary
of Montserrat. Look down
from these cliffs on the faithful, old earth:
ours, small, poor.

Seek yourself
on the long road of hope.
Venture along the path
of the hidden fountain.
Listen to water's
benign murmur.
Cut yourself on
the refound crystal of Grace.

May the ancient Virgin of the Mountain
always protect you.
And, as the days go by,
when you behold Her, remember me.

Fragment from a poem by Salvador Espriu (1913-1985), published in 1957 to mark the 75th anniversary of the coronation of the image of Our Lady of Montserrat.

A surprising world

Montserrat is a massif formed, basically, by material from the Tertiary Age. The highest peak in these mountains is Mount Sant Jeroni.

The pilgrim who walks up the mountain to the sanctuary, the stranger who discovers its beauty and spirituality for the first time, the worshipper who makes an offering to the patron saint, the guest who finds the longed-for retreat... all visitors will find in Montserrat an outstanding site where the geological formations encourage us to give free rein to our imaginations, where the holiness of the sanctuary fosters devotion, where culture finds sublime expression.

In Montserrat, nature, spirituality and culture join together to provide a transcendent visit that cannot fail to leave its mark. A truly unique mountain geographically, with its sawtooth aspect. A monastery founded more than one thousand years ago, the site of a universal sanctuary that symbolises the devotion of the Catalan people, whose patron saint is Our Lady of Montserrat. A historic heritage that is still very much alive today, present in institutions with centuries of tradition.

Nature

Geological formation

The idea of time that we best understand and apply in our day-to-day lives lies on a scale that goes from one year to a few thousand years, enabling us to understand our own history. In geology, however, such a period is merely a brief moment in the history of the Earth, and for this reason time is measured in more appropriate units, millions of years. In the approximately 3,760 million years of the Earth's geological history, what are now the

lands of Central Catalonia, in which Mount Montserrat lies, have existed for the last 50 million years. Over that time, in order to understand the formation of this massif, we need to speak about a great sea gulf, its waters not so deep, that existed during the Lower Eocene (50 million years ago), situated where we now find the Catalan Central Depression, into which flowed powerful rivers from the slopes of a Catalan-Balearic Massif (since disappeared) carrying huge masses of rocks. These rocks became mixed with softer, stickier substances (sand, clay and silt) to form a great mass of conglomerate, which is the stone that formed the Massif of Montserrat; geologically speaking, this rock is of

the detrital sedimentary type: rounded fragments whose origin lies in other, pre-existing rocks, broken off by erosion and deposited as sediment once again, in our case by calcareous cement. Scientifically, this rock is known as "pudding stone".

Around 35 million years ago, this marine gulf began to shrink, eventually drying up completely, and the marine basin became a continental basin. Later, some 20 million years ago, the folding of the Pyrenees, due to the action of tectonic forces, raised all these sediments to the surface, creating a more or less uniform massif.

The present form of the mountain is the result of a combination of two main factors: erosion caused by weathering (particularly by water) and the existence of a network of vertical fractures (technically known as joints), which affects the entire massif. Water percolates down into these fractures, gradually dissolving the calcium carbonate that forms part of conglomerates, creating the Karst morphol-

ogies of our mountain: terrestrial forms caused by water through erosive processes. The result is the formation of caves and potholes.

This combination of factors all helped to shape the characteristic relief of Mount Montserrat. Examples of these forms include the peak of Sant Jeroni (1,236 m), the highest point in the massif. Separate from Mt Sant Jeroni by the col known as the Coll de Migdia, we find Els Ecos (1,220m). Coll de Migdia, at the centre of which rises spiky Talaia,

divides the sierra into two almost equal parts: the eastern section, encompassing the Santa Magdalena area and the sierras of Santa Maria, Sant Salvador and Els Flautats, including the well-known monolith known as Cavall Bernat (1,111m); and the western section, the zone embracing Els Ecos, Els Frares Encantats ("The Enchanted Friars") and Les Agulles ("The Needles"), including the peculiar Coll de Port col.

Some of the archaeological remains found in the three main caves in the massif, reproduced in the book Prehistòria de Montserrat *("Prehistory of Montserrat"), published by Monestir de Montserrat in 1925.*

Montserrat has inspired both the popular imagination and the works of main writers and artists.

Environment

Vegetation

Mount Montserrat is, above all, an area populated by holm-oak woods. Despite the immediate impression of a rocky wilderness, once we begin to explore the paths around the massif we quickly discover how abundant the vegetation on the flats and, particularly, in the channels. Due to the peculiar ecological conditions here, we also find many endemic species on scarps and rocky areas.

The mean maximum temperature is 17.2°, whilst the mean minimum is 9.8°. Although the climate is typically Mediterranean, the dense arboreal stratum formed by the holm-oak woods creates undergrowth that is rather more humid, enabling bushes and lianas to grow profusely. These species include: Mediterranean buckthorn, sarsaparilla, viburnum, honeysuckle, broom, box, ivy and arbutus, amongst many others. Broadly speaking, we can differentiate between the holm-oak woods on the lower slopes of the mountain, up to 600-700m (or 1,000m on the sunny side) as holm-oak woods with viburnum, and those situated over 600 m in the shade as holm-oak woods with box. In the former, we find rosemary and thyme, whilst the holm-oak woods with box and north-facing rocks are inhabited by communities of saxifrage and starflowers, species that are practically endemic in Montserrat.

Wildlife

Due to human pressure around the mountain area, a situation worsened by a large forest fire in 1986, wildlife populations, particularly as regards larger species, are falling. Generally speaking, the species found today are all typically Mediterranean.

Damp winds from the sea often cause thick mist on the mountains, creating a beneficial climate for the growth of the endemic flora.

Limestone saxifrage (Saxifraga callosa).

Spanish ibex.

Pyrenean violet (Ramonda Myconi).

Bonelli's eagle.

Overall view of the massif from the Monistrol side.

"The Needles".

"The Pregnant Lady" and "The Elephant's Trunk".

View of "The Needles".

"The Mummy", "The Little Mummy", "The Pepper", "The Nightwatchman", "The Nightwatchman's Whistle" and "The Fourth of Trinity".

Chapel of Sant Joan.

Viewpoint of Sant Miquel.

Cavall Bernat is, in fact, more than a needle, a sierra. This "Horse Bernard" is located on the northern side of eastern Montserrat, over Monistrol. From the peak to the foot of Cavall Bernat is a sheer fall of 245 metres of conglomerate rock, whilst the needle rises some 60 metres over the crest. The needle was climbed for the first time in 1935.
On the peak is a statue of Our Lady (partial view in box).

‹ *The area known as the "Enchanted Friars".*

"The Needles".

"The Hollow Rock" and "The Little Chair".

View of the east face. >

"The Dead Man's Head".

"Gorro Frigi".

The Tebaia Sierra. In the background, "The Mummy" and "The Elephant's Trunk".

Many caves and chasms appear due to geological formation of the rocks.

Portal from the old Romanesque Church of Santa Maria (12th century).

The Monastery of Santa Cecília, a building with a basilica ground plan of three parallel naves, with cannon vault, completed by semicircular apse. The central nave, longer than the others, is projected towards the west and is joined to the side aisles by two semicircular arches.

Geographic and administrative territory

Although its evident geographic unity and peculiar geological and geomorphological characteristics, the Massif of Montserrat forms part of the Serralada Prelitoral Catalan, a chain that stretches between the Central and Prelitoral depressions of Central Catalonia. The mountain is 10 km long and 5 km wide, its 25 km perimeter straddling Bages, Anoia and Baix Llobregat counties. The mountain encompasses four municipalities: Monistrol, Collbató, El Bruc and Marganell. Mount Montserrat was designated as a natural park in 1987.

Montserrat is a symbol of Catalonia.

Routes around the chapels

Since time immemorial, Montserrat has been a favourite site amongst hermits. The first indication that the anchoretic life had reached these mountains, having spread to the west from the east, date back to the 7th century, with a certain growth during the period of Moorish occupation (8th-9th centuries) and considerable consolidation after Wilfred the Hairy, Count of Barcelona, won these lands back from the Islamic armies.

Historically, there were twelve hermitages on Montserrat and, even though there were so few such sites, they were a key source of attraction to the pilgrims who ascended the mountain. Some 300 hermits are known, all of whom with their own individual histories, despite their attachment to the monastery. Some were illustrious figures, famed for their holiness, their writings and even for the posts they held, both before and after becoming hermits, particularly those who had previously been monks. The hermitages were abandoned during the French War in 1811 and although they were subsequently reconstructed, they finally fell into disuse in around 1822.

The chapels of Montserrat are an expression of spiritual life on the mountain.

Chapel of Sant Martí.

Geodesic dome at
Sant Jeroni.

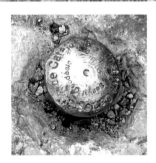

Chapel of Sant Dimas.

‹ Chapel of Sant Miquel.

Chapel of Sant Joan.

Chapel of the Holy Cave.

Partial view of the rock hermitage of Sant Onofre.

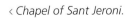

‹ *Chapel of Sant Jeroni.*

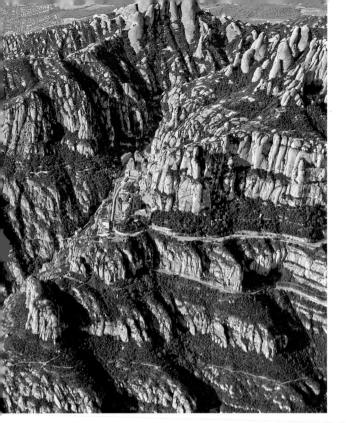

Pilgrim ways

Montserrat has always been sanctuary of devotion for thousands of pilgrims, some of them worshippers of great religious figures such as the Apostle Saint James or Saint Ignatius of Loyola.

The best known path is the Way of Saint James, historically linked to our country through the popular legend that the Apostle Saint James preached in several Catalan cities. Moreover, some of the first pilgrims on record were Catalan, including Abbot Cesari, founder of the Monastery of Santa Cecília de Montserrat in 942. There are on Catalan territory five Ways considered the most habitual, including two in particular. These two, which both lead here from Narbonne, are the routes for pilgrimages to Montserrat itself.

One of the most popular sections of the Way amongst pilgrims today is that from Montserrat to Igualada, a 25.7 km stretch that usually begins on the Degotalls Path towards Santa Cecília; another possible starting point is Collbató, taking Les Bat-

eries Path. Pilgrims taking the Way for religious or spiritual reasons and who wish to obtain the Compostelana certificate, which is issued at Santiago Cathedral can have their Credentials stamped at the Pastoral Coordination Centre in the Sanctuary of Montserrat.

Montserrat is also a principal sanctuary principal on the Way of Saint Ignatius, which follows the route that Ignatius of Loyola, when still a knight, took from Loyola to Manresa in 1522; this Way enables the devout to experience a pilgrimage that recreates the spiritual process that the Saint underwent. The Way ends at the Cave of Saint Ignatius in Manresa; the Montserrat section is, therefore, the last. On the night from 24 to 25 March 1522, the Saint offered his knight's sword before the image of Our Lady of Montserrat and dressed in the pilgrim's sackcloth. A copy of the sword can be seen in a display case in the Basilica of Montserrat, near the chapel devoted to Saint Ignatius. The sculpture of Saint Ignatius, by Rafel Solanic (1895-1990) in the basilica atrium recalls the night that the Saint spent praying to Our Lady. The round black marble slab before this sculpture marks the place where the altar of the old Romanesque church where Ignatius prayed.

During the times of Abbot Oliba, in around the year 1025, a group of monks from Ripoll built the Monastery of Santa Maria de Montserrat beside the Chapel of Santa Maria.

Coat of arms of Montserrat.

The monastery

A history spanning more than one thousand years

The origins

We have learned about the origins of Christian life in Montserrat, which goes back to the times of the first hermits, and how this presence became consolidated during the reign of Wilfred the Hairy, Count of Barcelona (840-897). We find the first documentary mention of Montserrat in 888 when the count donated a number of lands to the Monastery of Ripoll. These included: the churches of Montserrat, those that are on the mountain and those at the bottom, with their territory". These were the churches of Sant Iscle and Santa Maria, Sant Pere and Sant Martí.

Before the monks of Ripoll really began to occupy themselves with these churches on Montserrat, which now belonged to them, another group of monks took up dwelling on the mountain, led by Abbot Cesari in 942 at the Church of Santa Cecília, located 4 km from the present Monastery of Santa Maria. This abbot built a new church, more appropriate for the monastic liturgy that has largely survived down to the present. The church has a nave and two aisles, the latter shorter than the former, with three altars: that in the nave dedicated to Saint Cecilia, the aisle naves to Saint Mary and Saint Peter.

It was during the times of Abbot Oliba (971-1046), in around 1025, that a community of monks from Ripoll built the Monastery of Santa Maria de Montserrat, beside the original Church of Santa Maria.

The medieval period

During this period, the monastery became consolidated and expanded, still under the rule of Ripoll, but with ever-greater influence from the priors of Montserrat until, finally, the site became an abbey in 1409. Devotion to the image of Our Lady placed Montserrat at the epicentre of religious feeling in the region and, from that time on, the monks had the task of conserving this statue.

The closing years in this period were by no means easy, and, in the 15th century, saw a clear decline in the Benedictine monastic movement, which also affected Montserrat. The arrival of Abbot García de Cisneros in 1493 from the Monastery of San Benito in Valladolid, sent by the Catholic Monarchs, marked the beginning of a new period that stands out in the centuries-long history of the monastery.

The baroque period

The modern period was one of reforms and growth and the spread of a cultural heritage that crossed borders. The abbots of this period left a mark that is still present at Montserrat even today, in its architecture, building the new church and other monastic buildings, and in its culture, through the music of the boys' choir and many incunables made at the monastery (1499-1500).

Saint Benedict.

Aerial views of the mountain and the monastery.

The "Drummer of El Bruc".

The arrival of the contemporary era was marked by tragedy for the monastery: in 1811 the Napoleonic troops set fire to and pillaged Montserrat during the Spanish War of Independence.

Unfortunately, most of the material heritage produced during this period has since been lost, due to the events that came to pass in the early-19th century.

The contemporary period

The contemporary period reached the monastery marked by tragedy: in 1811, during the War of Independence, Napoleonic troops sacked and burned Montserrat. The process of liberalisation, which occupied the whole of the 19th century, including the disentailment of 1835, greatly conditioned but could not halt the material and spiritual reconstruction of Montserrat, which became a reality in 1881, when Our Lady of Montserrat was proclaimed Patron Saint of Catalonia during the Millennium Festival. Our Lady was also crowned at this time (the crown is now on public display in the Museum of Montserrat).

Those choosing to reach the monastery by train have two options: the cable car up to the monastery or the rack railway. In the photo, the arrivals at the Monasteryterminal.

During the 20th century, the community was also forced to over come tragic events (such as the dispersal of the community itself and the death of 23 monks during the Spanish Civil War) and to play a role as a symbol and refuge of Catalan culture and rights. Landmarks include celebrations for the installation of the holy image on a silver throne, paid for by public subscription, on 27 April 1947. Another important event in the 20th century was the pilgrimage to the site made by Pope John Paul II on 7 November 1982.

The monastery today

Montserrat along its historic path and is preparing to celebrate the thousandth year of its foundation as a monastery in 2025. The present community, formed by some sixty monks, is devoted, as always, to a life of prayer, work and welcoming the thousands of pilgrims who come to the Sanctuary every year.

The liturgy marks the daily rhythm of the monastic life, from daybreak to day's end. Every day, the monks come together six times to celebrate the Liturgy of the Hours and to take communion, the

The cable-car trip from the "Aeri de Montserrat" railway station to the monastery takes 5 minutes and you can take in some breathtaking views on the way.

The views from the train are absolutely spectacular.

central act in the day-to-day life of the monastery and the sanctuary. Many pilgrims also attend these services.

The community also performs great pastoral work: conducting services in the basilica, welcoming groups, recesses and conferences, and attending to accommodation services. Besides the work necessary for the good functioning of monastery life, there are also monks devoted to tasks in a wide variety of fields. To mention but one, great importance has always been attached here to Bible studies, a field in which outstanding achievements include the translation of the Bible into Catalan and its interpretation.

Many, varied and important are the institutions related to Montserrat that are directed by one of the

View from the rack railway.

The rack railway station.

monks. Examples include the Museum of Montserrat, the Choir, the Library and Publications of Montserrat Abbey. This publishing company, which disseminates Catalan culture, has operated practically without interruption since 1499 at the services of the Sanctuary and Monastery of Montserrat. The publishing arm has produced more than 3,000 titles on a range of subjects including history, art, essay, studies of language and literature, religion, music, hiking and books for children and younger readers. Besides books, the company also publishing around a dozen magazines, including *Serra d'Or, Qüestions de Vida Cristiana* and *Studia Monastica*.

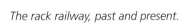
The rack railway, past and present.

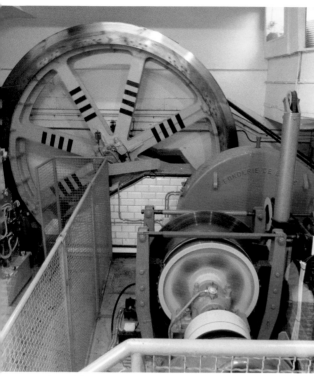

The cable car traction mechanism.

The Sant Joan cable car.
Partial view of the route.

The Holy Cave cable car.

View of the site from inside the Sant Joan cable car station.

Areas of the monastery

The library

As a Benedictine monastery, Montserrat houses as an essential tool for work and culture; the li-brary, which occupies a central place on the mo-nastic site. Since the very origins of the order, the Benedictines have always mentioned books as necessary instruments for the monk's spiritual and intellectual formation. A monolith at the library en-trance reminds us that: "The library is an indispen-sable part of a Benedictine monastery". For this reason, the monastery is known to have conserved manuscripts since the site was first founded, and in the 11th century Montserrat had its own scriptorium, a place devoted to study and making written copies. This scriptorium was very active in the 14th and 15th centuries. The installation of a print shop at Montserrat under the aegis of Abbot Cisneros in 1499, the origin of the present publishing company, also contributed to the work of cultural dissemination undertaken by the monastery. In the 17th and 18th centuries, the library grew and its collections were diversified until it conserved, it appears, thousands of works. The destruction that took place in 1811 included the loss of most of this bibliographic treasure.

The present library was founded in the late-19th century and grew particularly during the abbacy of Father Antoni Marcet (1912-1939). In the space of just a few years, the collection increased from 16,000 volumes to a figure of approximately 50,000. The period marked by the Spanish Civil War and the Second World War made further growth impossible in those times, but the collections have doubled in size over the last few decades.

The particularly outstanding sections include those devoted to philosophy, theology, Bible studies, patristics, liturgy, music and art history. Also noteworthy are those dedicated to universal general history, especially the medieval period and Europe, Catalonia and the Crown of Aragon, with a including many works on local history and the Spanish Civil War. The catalogue includes: 330,000 monographs, 6,000 periodicals, 1,500 manuscripts, 400 incunables, 3,700 books from the 16th century, 18,000 engravings and 500 historic maps. Of all the manuscripts, particularly outstanding is the *Lli-*

The library.

bre Vermell or Red Book, written in Montserrat in the 14th and 15th centuries and comprising a miscellany of theological and devotional texts, as well as others devoted to geographic, cultural and social questions. Also noteworthy is a folio containing a fragment from the *Forum Iudicum*, a 12th-century Catalan translation of a compilation of Visigoth laws, and one of the first known texts in Catalan.

The Chapter House

The Chapter House is the place where the community gathers officially to receive doctrine from the abbot or to celebrate deliberative and elective sessions. Altered in 1940, the present Chapter House is decorated as a whole in noble, austere style. The painter Pere Pruna (1904-1977) later added the mural paintings devoted to the theme

The Chapter House. >

The library.

The Chapter House.

of the monks who died during the Spanish Civil War (1936-1939).

Monastic life unfolds in a family environment, the community sharing both spiritual and material goods, in a quest to live the Christian life according to the Rule of Saint Benedict and under the guidance of the abbot. The text of the Rule, which was written by Benedict of Nursia in Italy in the 6th century, outlines the principles of monastic life and, in short, comprises an initiation into the Christian life, urging monks to follow Christ unconditionally under the guidance of the Gospel. The text was adopted as the basis of western monasticism during much of the Middle Ages; structured into 74 chapters, the text even permits an interpretation adapted to the present times.

The fraternal atmosphere amongst the community embodies a spirit of dialogue and mutual communication so that each member of the community is co-responsible for the good running of the monastery, helping the abbot in all decisions that have to be taken. The Chapter House is used for such moments of deliberation, judgment and decision making at community level and also for addresses that the abbot regularly makes to the monastic community.

Near the to Chapter House is the so-called the Room of the Sign, where the Benedictine monks form rows by strict order, with the seniors at the front and the last to have entered the monastery at the back. This is a place where the historical memory of the monastery is conserved. Besides the statue of Saint Benedict Legislator, the room also contains the cenotaph of the founder, Abbot Oliba, and the reformer García de Cisneros. The Room of the Sign also houses the monastery obituary, that is to say, the book recording the anniversaries of monks deceased at the monastery, which is read out daily. Over the centuries, it is estimated that around 2,500 monks have lived at Montserrat.

The cloister

The interior cloister at the monastery communicates several rooms and dependencies. However, above all, it gives coherence to an internal space that is made irregular due to the difficult terrain of the mountain. This cloister was built by architect Josep Puig i Cadafalch (1867-1956) in 1925 and is considered Romanesque Revival in style, though it is in perfect harmony with the *noucentista* ("19th-century") architecture that Abbot Marcet championed during his abbacy (1912-1939). The cloister is formed by two stories of brick arches supported by stone columns; all along the walls are many archaeological and lapidary pieces, important for their historic and artistic value, dating from the 10th to the 18th century.

The ground floor, which features a shrine with fountain in the centre, evoking the great monastic cloisters of Catalonia, leads into the garden,

The cloister and the shrine.

where the community members can find a peaceful atmosphere that invites them to thought and tranquillity. In this garden stands the 12th-century Chapel of Sant Iscle, one of the four small churches mentioned in the document dating to the year 888, its Romanesque structure well conserved. Also noteworthy is the marble sculpture of *The Good Shepherd* by Manolo Hugué (1872-1945). This sculpture was made in 1944 to honour the memory of two monks who died in the Spanish Civil War. A plaster copy of this sculpture, by the same artist, is currently on show in the Museum of Montserrat.

Font in the cloister shrine.

Partial view.

Tomb of Prior Ramon de Vilagut.

Cloister: lower gallery.

The refectory

Meal times are important moments in community life; the Bible itself emphasises the spiritual dimension and teaches us that God is present in the communion amongst those breaking bread together. That is why monasticism imbues meals with an almost liturgical atmosphere, as they begin and end with prayer and are taken in silence. Moreover, besides the body, the spirit is also nurtured by the reading that accompanies meals. The Rule of Saint Benedict ordains that: "Reading must not be wanting at the table of the brethren when they are eating". That is why the throne occupies a special place in the middle of the room.

The refectory at Montserrat was renovated by the architect Puig i Cadafalch in 1925, whose reforms achieved, particularly, good lighting in the room. Puig i Cadafalch also designed the tables and chairs here. An important change was made in 1960: the Rule also specifies: "Let the Abbot's table always be with the guests and travellers". With this rule in mind, the high area was reorganised with tables forming a circle, and the monastery's guests dine at these tables.

The refectory.

The Sanctuary
The presence of the Holy Image

The unique and special beauty of Mount Montserrat, with its majestic spires soaring skywards, make this the ideal site for manifesting the presence of the religious message. No doubt the monks who arrived here in the 11th century felt the call of this holy place, urging them to conserve and watch over the sanctuary dedicated to Our Lady.

The maximum expression of this devotion is found in the holy image of Our Lady of Montserrat, venerated over the centuries and popularly known as "La Moreneta" ("The Black Madonna") due to Her dark colour. The image of Our Lady of Montserrat is a gilded polychrome Romanesque carving dating to the late-12th century, though the hands of both Mary and Baby Jesus had to be replaced as a consequence of the damaged caused during the aforementioned French War (1811-12).

The holy image follows the iconographic model of The Virgin in Majesty, or *Sedes Sapientiae* ("The Throne of Wisdom"), which became most popular during the Romanesque period. In it, Our Lady is seated, with the Child on Her lap, in a regal, frontal, highly hieratic pose. In Her right hand, Our Lady holds the orb, or sphere of the universe, whilst with her left she makes a gesture to protect the Child.

The Infant gives a blessing with His right hand whilst, in His left, He holds a pineapple (in the original version He had held an orb), a perennial fruit, sign of fertility and eternal life. Around His neck is a border with a brooch like that of His Mother, and he is wearing a tunic and over-tunic with the same decoration. He is bare-footed, whilst His mother is

wearing shoes, her feet resting on a cushion that acts as a footstool.

The colour of the face and hands of this Virgin, with Her serene and austere beauty, is most likely due to slow transformation, a process of the oxidation of varnish made from white lead and the action of smoke from many candles and oil lamps that burned near the altar in this tiny Romanesque church for many years. From Her throne in Montserrat, Mary is worshipped by countless thousands who flock here from all around the world.

The image of the Madonna and Child, symbolising God's love for humanity, is found in several sites in the Sanctuary.

The Way of the Holy Cave.

The Boys' Choir. >

The legend of the discovery of Our Lady of Montserrat

According to legend, in the year 880 when some pastors from the town of Monistrol brought their flocks to graze on Mount Montserrat. Suddenly, as it was getting dark, the shepherds saw a great light and heard heavenly singing, wondrous signs that pointed to a place on the mountain. Amazed, they told their story to the priest and of the neighbouring parish, who repeated their tale to the bishop. Subsequently, bishop and villagers went in awe and devotion to the site of the miracle. The beam of light was coming from a cave in which, sheltered under a cliff, they found the holy image.

As this place was steep and inaccessible, they decided to take the image to Manresa, the largest nearby city but, as the party crossed the stream to reach a plateau protected from the north winds, the Virgin wrought another miracle: the statue became completely immobile and unmovable, so that everyone realised that this was the place that She had chosen to be worshipped. Our Lady loved that place, and from there wished to call to Her devoted children to take the path of penance and conversion.

Montserrat Boys' Choir

We must seek the origins of the Montserrat Boys' Choir in the educational vocation of religious institutions in the Middle Ages; the existence of the Montserrat Boys' Choir is documented as far back as the 13th century. Canons' colleges in cathedrals and communities of monks in monasteries performed educational work at the service of the society of those times. In the case of the monks, the presence of song and music as an essential element of the liturgy explains their specialisation in music schools. This is the context within which we should understand the Montserrat Boys' Choir, although the fact that it continues to exist even today makes it a unique case, for its members are trained at one of the oldest music schools in Europe.

The sheet music to Virolai, the hymn devoted to Our Lady of Montserrat, written by Jacint Verdaguer.

At present, there are about forty children aged between eight and fourteen (treble voices) in the choir. They sing the *Salve* and the *Virolai* at 1 pm from Monday to Friday, and take part in the Conventual Mass on Sundays at 12 noon; from Sunday to Thursday they also take part in evening prayers at 6.45 pm. In recent years, moreover, the choir has given major concerts worldwide, converting the Boys' Choir into an ambassador for Montserrat and Catalan culture around the globe.

Virolai is a hymn dedicated to Our Lady of Montserrat whose first verse begins with the lines "*Rosa d'abril, Morena de la serra, de Montserrat estel*" ("Rose of April, Dark Lady of the Mountains, Star of Montserrat"), and the piece is also therefore known as *Rosa d'abril*. The words of *Virolai* are by the poet Jacint Verdaguer (1845-1902) and were published in the programme for the art and music competition held as part of celebrations for the Millennium of Montserrat in 1880. The Master Josep Rodoreda (1851-1922) won the competition for best popular melody adapted to Verdaguer's text in that same year, 1880.

This great musical tradition of Montserrat is also evident in musicians and composers from the so-called *Escola Montserratina*, a school always linked to the children's choir. In the golden age of the baroque, the outstanding figures included Anselm Viola (1738-1798) and Narcís Casanoves (1747-1799), amongst others; whilst in contemporary times we should mention Father Àngel Rodamilans (1874-1936). Similarly important are the contributions made by great musicians to the repertoire of the choir here; these include, particularly, the Catalan cellist and composer Pau Casals (1876-1973), who composed such pieces as *Nigra Sum* and *Cançó a la Verge* for the Montserrat Boys' Choir.

Views of Montserrat Boys' Choir.

The portal in the main façade of the Basilica.

The white and grey pavement in the atrium, designed by Father Benet Martínez. The medallion and the inscription reveal its symbolism: only the baptised shall understand the meaning of the Eucharistic fish. ›

The basilica

The atrium

This space is bounded by the Abbot Benet Argerich building, constructed in the 18th century to provide accommodation for the monks, and which we now see from the inside. The atrium is formed by two cloisters that stand before the church, following its axis. This was a great improvement for the monastery, with two spacious cloisters in front of the church fulfilling the function of an atrium, and six stories of rooms for the monks in the south wing.

With its thick walls, this is a work that survived the destruction that took place Montserrat in 1811 reasonably well. In 1952, the atrium was altered to change its austere appearance and make this a transitional space between the profane and the sacred domains. Particularly outstanding features include the floor, designed by Father Benet Martinez (1918-1988), which reproduces the design that Michelangelo created for the Campidoglio in Rome; its symbolic interpretation is found in the central medallion and in the inscription around it: only the baptised, who are born in water like fish, will understand what eating the Eucharist fish means. These reforms are completed by the sgraffito work designed by Josep Obiols (1894-1967) for the three façades, and several large Solomonic or barley-sugar columns in the *noucentista* ("19th-century") style.

The atrium area also contains the baptistery, placed separately from the church in accordance with the

The atrium.

Partial view of the basilica façade. Sculptures of Jesus and the Apostles, by Agapit Vallmitjana.

Entrance to the basilica atrium. Sculptures of His Holiness Pope Pius X, Saint Ignatius of Loyola, Saint Anthony Mary Claret and King Charles V.

ancient liturgy. This is another contemporary work (1958), its most interesting features including the sculptural facade made by the Swiss artist Charles Collet (1902-1983), depicting the mystery of the church that, through the sacraments, blesses the lives and activities of men and women.

Embedded in a side wall in the atrium, we can see the old Romanesque portal, the only remnant from the old church that has survived to our day. Although badly damaged, the portal, which dates back to the last quarter of the 12th century, is adorned by sumptuous decoration: formed by five semicircular archivolts, the atrium features a capital depicting the themes of the Creation and sin of Adam and Eve.

The facade of the church that we see today was inaugurated in 1901 and was designed by the architect Villar Carmona. This is a great neo-Plateresque feature, its historicist style inspired by the Spanish Plateresque art, a movement that marked the transition from the Gothic to the Renaissance (15th-17th centuries). The decoration includes sculptures of Jesus Christ and the Twelve Apostles, by Agapit Vallmitjana (1830-1905), whilst the reliefs in the three tympana are the work of his brother, Venanci Vallmitjana (1826-1919). In the central door, Pope Leo XIII receives Bishop Urquinaona, who asks the Holy Father to proclaim Our Lady of Montserrat as patron saint of Catalonia. The door on the right represents the Birth of Mary, that on the left, the Dormition.

< *The old Romanesque door.*

The construction of the new church

Work on the present church began in 1560, and the site was consecrated in 1592. This is a project linked to Abbot Bartomeu Garriga (1559-1562 – 1568-1570). The church occupies a space where the monastery was originally planned for construction, but was finally built here due to the need to replace the old Romanesque building, which had been rendered too small to accommodate the many faithful and also to the needs of the monastic offices. The style of this church can be described as transitional between the Gothic and the Renaissance, and its architectural importance resides mainly in its monumental quality.

In 1811, during the French War, the church was burned down by the French army, and it was razed once more in 1812, as well as destroyed by explosives, which reduced it completely to a pile of ruins. Although reconstruction began immediately, it was not until 1872, in the time of Abbot Muntades (1858-1885) and in accordance with plans drawn up by the architect Francisco de Paula del Villar Lozano (1828-1901), that an ambitious large-scale restoration project was undertaken. However, the period of maximum was under Abbot Deàs (1885-1913). The architect's plans were based on adopting a medieval-influenced style, one that Villar himself described as neo-Byzantine style. In 1881, during the papacy of Leo XIII, the Church of Montserrat was consecrated as a basilica.

Between 1991 and 1996, the basilica was restored again, externally and internally. The main features in this latest restoration include the completion of the dome, never previously built, and which, with the portholes, improves the lighting inside.

Offerings to Our Lady on the Ave Maria Way.

Offerings to Our Lady.

Angel of the Annunciation.

Large candles that burn constantly, made from the remains of those offered by pilgrims.

Partial views of the Ave Maria Way.

The present chapels

The Church of Montserrat measures 68.32 m in length, 21.50 m in width and 33.20 m in height. The building is formed by a single nave with six side chapels on either flank, arranged between the buttresses; over these side chapels are galleries. The chapels, destroyed in 1811, were largely reformed during the time of Abbot Deàs, an intervention involving mainly artists linked to the Art Nouveau movement, known as Modernism in Catalonia. The most recent renovation of two chapels also saw the introduction of

contemporary art to the site, and contemporary art is also reflected in the large number of votive lamps distributed throughout the basilica; although this tradition comes from medieval times, in the belief that a lamps kept alight ensured the enduring presence of the devout at the feet of the Our Lady, the present lamps date from 1947 and later. Some were made by precious metalworkers and enamellers of the highest standing. All are catalogued, and in the basilica we see notes providing information has to who offered them, the year and the artist.

Votive lamps.

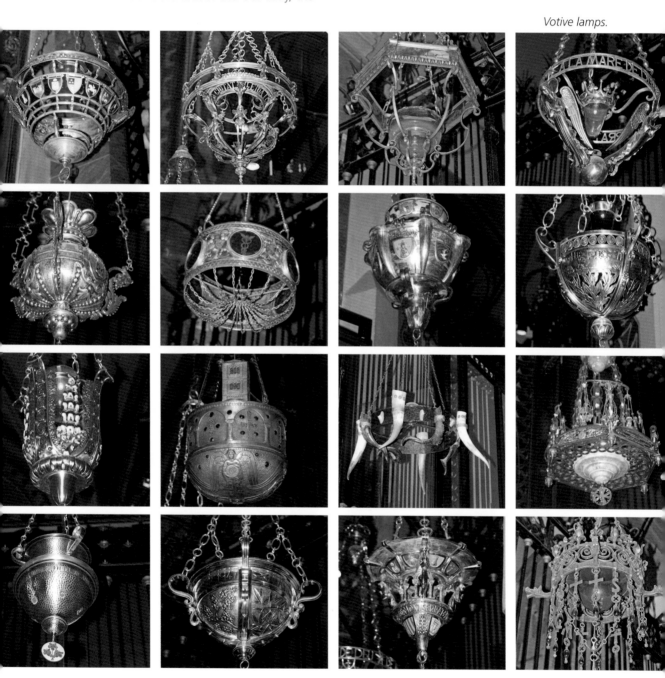

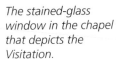
Altar of Saint Joseph of Calasanz, a magnificent modernist work by Francesc Berenguer i Mestres in 1891. Berenguer was a follower and associate of Gaudí, whose influence can be observed in certain features of the altar.

The stained-glass window in the chapel that depicts the Visitation.

Saint Benedict, in a painting by Montserrat Gudiol.

Side chapels (right)

On this side, in the first chapel contains a statue of Saint Peter, by Josep Viladomat (1899-1989), evoking the famous sculpture in Saint Peter's Basilica.

In the second is the Altar of Saint Ignatius, designed by architect Francesc Rogent (1861-1898) in 1893. Particularly interesting here is the fine sculpture by Venanci Vallmitjana (1828-1919), representing Pope Saint Clement.

The third is the Chapel of Saint Martin, with Gothic Revival designed by Joan Riera and sculpture by Josep Llimona in 1896. Here, the sculptor depicts the scene when the Roman soldier rips his chlamys in two to cover a poor naked person, and in which he inserted a self-portrait. Added to flank this piece on either side were statues of saints Placidus and Maurus, and the chapel ornamentation is completed by a superb, decorative mural painting.

In the fourth chapel is a monumental altarpiece dedicated to Saint Joseph Calasanz, who spent an important formative period at Montserrat, paid for by the Pious Schools, in 1891 and the work of Francesc Berenguer i Mestres (1866-1914), a close associate of Gaudí. This altarpiece is in the full Art Nouveau or Modernist style, as we can appreciate in the stylised plant motifs, the use of floral decoration against a gilt background and the ironwork features that complete the altar.

The last chapel is dedicated to Saint Benedict; it was renovated in 1980, which marked 1,500 years since the birth of the saint. Here, Montserrat Gudiol (1933) painted a young Benedict (using as her seventeen-year-old son as the model), moving confidently forward, holding in his hand the book of the Rule. The composition is resolved in black and bluish gray, whilst the figure, reduced to flesh, is transfigured by a light from within.

Side aisle with chapels devoted chapels.

The Chapel of the Holy Sacrament was refurbished in 1977. The sculptural work is by Josep María Subirachs, the goldwork is by Manuel Capdevila and the liturgical furniture is by Joaquim Capdevila. The apparent sobriety of the altar is complemented by the rich iconographic setting: over the altarpiece, the Risen Christ is represented only by an embossed image of His face, with hands and feet marked by nails and His side with the wound of the spear, while on the altar frontispiece is a bare thighbone, symbolising death.

Side chapels (left)

On the mountain side, the first chapel is the Altar of the Immaculate Conception, designed by Josep M. Pericas (1881-1965) in excellent modernist style due to the young architect's careful observation of the great masters of this movement when he took on the project (1910). The decorative motifs are inspired by the organic world of plants and animals. The central sculpture features the Immaculate wearing a royal crown with inlaid mother-of-pearl; flanking Her are saints Raymond Nonnatus and Joseph Oriol. On the front wall of the chapel is a statue of Saint Emilio: members of the family that funded the work were named after these saints. We can also see some splendid stained glass here, designed by the painter Darius Vilàs (1880-1950). Overall, this chapel is one of the most beautiful and harmonious in the whole basilica.

The second is the Chapel of the Holy Christ, which features a statue by Josep Llimona (1864-1934) donated in 1933 by the Bearers of the Holy Christ in the bishopric of Barcelona.

Presiding over the third chapel, which is dedicated to the Holy Family, is the painting *The Flight into Egypt*, by Josep Cusachs (1851-1908). This work, dated 1904, was the result of a commission from a Spanish family living in New York, stipulating that Cusachs should donate the painting to Montserrat. In it, the painter portrays himself as Saint Joseph and his wife as Mary. The result is a fine example of a religious theme interpreted in accordance with the modernist naturalism of the time.

The largest chapel is that of the Blessed Sacrament, since this was converted into a "sunken" chapel in the seventeenth century and its apse is formed by the very rock of the mountain. In 1977, when the monks Pere Busquets (an architect) and Pere Crisòleg Picas decided to renovate the chapel, they commissioned Subirachs to create the sculpture for it. Overall, this chapel exudes an impressive austerity combined with extraordinary expressive power. The chapel is formed by a continuous concrete structure that forms the altar, the credence table, the tabernacle and a vertical altarpiece, above which are only the face, hands and feet of Christ, seen in negative, whilst His wounds are sensed as marks on the concrete. The verticality of the altarpiece contrasts with the horizontality of the stark femur symbolising death, embedded in the altar frontal.

The decoration in the Chapel of the Blessed Sacrament is completed by the frieze over the door, which is visible from the exterior. Made in bronze and designed as a railing, this frieze extends on either side of the glass door that connects the chapel with the nave of the basilica. The frieze is adorned by a narrative that imitates those over the lintels in medieval cathedrals representing heaven and hell,

Chapel of the Holy Christ

although the artist has applied his own personal symbolism. This is based on different dichotomies: good and evil, life and death, reason and chaos. All these elements form an iconography based on the confrontation of opposites; each symbol of evil is opposed by one of good, establishing a balance. The chapel is that of Santa Scholastica, dating to 1886 and adorned by sculptures by Enric Clarasó (1851-1941) and Agapit Vallmitjana (1830-1941). All Benedictine abbeys pay homage to Saint Benedict's twin sister, seen here as an abbess, with staff and pectoral cross. The side sculptures, by Vallmitjana, represent the penitent Saint Mary Magdalene and Saint Anthony of Padua.

View of the nave with the chapels radiating around it.

Chapel of Saint Scholastica.

Chapel of the Holy Family.

Chapel of the Immaculate Conception

Upper choir. Stalls.

The upper choir

Communicating with the galleries, which are placed over the last two sections of the nave, is the choir, an enormously important importance space in a monastic church. Today, however, the choir is only used during the nocturnal hours: Matins at 6 am, before sunrise, and Compline at 9.15 pm, before going to sleep. The monks prefer to pray the daytime hours in the lower choir, together with the congregation: Lauds at 7:30 am and Vespers at 6.45 pm. The same is true of Conventual Mass, the central liturgical act of the day, which takes place at 11 am.

The present choirstalls date to 1828 and were designed by the architect Antoni Cellers (1775-1835) and funded thanks to a donation by King Ferdinand VII. The architect employed the Ionic order for the columns of higher order and concentrated all the decoration on carvings of fantastic winged beasts that separate the seats.

Over the choir is the beautiful stained-glass rose window in the façade. Designed by Enric Monserdà (1848-1918) in 1894, this window sits on the central axis that connects with the holy image, and explains its mystery: Our Lady of Montserrat is the queen of heaven, and as such, is crowned by the Holy Trinity; the crown depicted here is that given as an offering in 1881, currently on display in the precious metalwork section of the Museum of Montserrat.

Partial view of the rose window.

Upper choir. Partial view of the stalls.

The presbytery and the high altar

The presbytery of the nave is polygonal in form; the gilt decoration and the so-called "triumphal arch of Mary", designed by the architect Villar, was installed in 1889. There are three canopies, the central featuring the image of Our Lady, flanked by the Archangels Saint Michael and Saint Gabriel. The presbytery is the space that precedes the high altar and is occupied, generally, by the choir. The presbytery at Montserrat was renovated in 1957 in accordance with more participatory and modern criteria, and which the Second Vatican Council (1962-65) later adopted for the whole Church. The project also was carried out by the aforementioned monks Father Pere Crisòleg Picas and Father Pere Busquets.

A year after this, a new altar was built from a block of conglomerate from Mount Montserrat. The frontal of this altar is adorned by silver and enamels, the work of Montserrat Mainar (1928): this adornment revives the old tradition of ennobling the central point of worship with precious metalwork: there are in Catalonia numerous examples of Romanesque frontals, although these, in polychrome wood, do not feature such noble materials. The centre of the frontal represents the Last Supper, whilst on the left is the scene of the loaves and fishes and on the right is the Wedding at Cana; at the ends are two angels, one in the robes of a deacon carrying the unleavened bread, the other dressed as a monk with censer.

In 1959, a magnificent cross in precious metal by Manuel Capdevila (1910-2006) was given as an offering to preside over the high altar of the basilica. That same artist also made the black silver canopy that crowns the altar in 1961. The figure of Christ is a beautiful Italian work dating back to the 16th century, already owned by the monastery at the time when the renovation work was undertaken.

The mural paintings

Particularly impressive features in the presbytery are there mural paintings, one of the finest ensembles in Catalan modernism (Art Nouveau); they were produced between 1896 and 1897 by members of the Sant Lluc Artists' Circle. The horizontal boxes on the bottom row represent, from left to right, the Pentecost, painted by Dionís Baixeras (1862-1943), the Assumption of Mary, by Lluís Graner (1863-1929), the Birth of Our Lady and the Presentation in the Temple, both by Joan Llimona (1860-1926).

Altar mayor, canopy and marble Christ. Above, in the background, the Shrine.

Alexandra de Riquer (1856-1920) painted the large vertical canvases nearest to Our Lady, clearly modernist works representing two angel hosts, as well as the other two panels with their floral motifs and heraldic emblems; that on the left is dedicated to Montserrat, that on the right is an exaltation of the Roman pontificate and the Benedictine Order. The two large panels nearest to the nave depict the legend behind the discovery of the holy image: that on the left, the scene of the shepherds, and that on the right the moment when the statue became immobile; the landscapes are by Joaquim Vancells (1866-1942), whilst the figures of the shepherds are by Dionís Baixeras and those of the procession by Joan Llimona. These paintings were made in between 1895 and 1897, during the time of Abbot Administrator Father Antoni Ruera, whilst Abbot Deàs was travelling on a mission to the Philippines. Father Ruera also commissioned the sculptures of the four major prophets installed in the nave of the basilica, the work of Josep Llimona (1864-1934), and which feature the texts of the prophecies referring to the Mother of God.

The stained glass in the large rose window in the basilica, designed by Enric Montserdà and made at the Amigó brothers' workshop in 1894. The work depicts the Coronation of Our Lady. The crown was donated by the Catalan people in 1881 to mark Her proclamation as the country's patron saint. The outstanding features include the magnificent colour range and the harmonious composition of the figures.

Stained-glass windows in the chapels representing different Bible scenes.

Partial views of the nave.

Crypt with sarcophagus carved by Joan Rebull containing the mortal remains of Abbot Marcet.

The crypt

A small staircase on the right-hand side of the presbytery, next to the Niche, leads down into the crypt. Due to the topography of the mountain, the crypt is not located beneath the altar, but in a space created by the downward slope of the rock. The room, austere and harmonious, with a barrel vault built in 1951, is the burial place of Abbot Marcet and the monks who were martyred in the Spanish Civil War.

The new organ

The new organ of Montserrat is installed in a space near the presbytery, located what is known as the Chapel of the Sacristy, on the side of the epistle. The organ is located here in response to the liturgical need to accompany the singing and the desire to preserve the tradition of the Catalan organ placed to one side, elevated over the nave and near the choir. This organ, inaugurated in 2010, was constructed at the Blancafort workshop in the nearby town of Collbató. It has 4,242 pipes, and measures 12.5 m in height and weighs about 12,000 kilos.

Thanks to its outstanding technical qualities, the new instrument is imbued with enormous potential for interpretation, covering a wide repertoire of organ music. It should be noted that the organ at Montserrat is one of the most frequently used, not only at the liturgical hours, but also in organ concert seasons organised here.

The organ.

The Boy's Choir.

Partial views of the organ.

The Niche of Our Lady

The Throne of the Holy Image

The construction of the throne entailed a complete renovation of the entrances, which was carried out by the architect Francesc Folguera. On entering, we first come to the "Angel Door", which communicates the basilica with the staircase to the Niche. The alabaster main arch, adorned by angel musicians, was installed in 1946; two years later, the remaining decoration was completed, with reliefs forming a triumphal arch; at the bottom are patriarchs and prophets from the Old Testament, while the upper section is devoted to the theme of "Maria Full of Grace". The tympanum evoking the eternal pre-existence of Mary in God's thought was installed in 1954. Acting as a prolongation of this triumphal arch, the steps that the pilgrim ascends are adorned by two retinues of two female characters: the saintly mothers on the left and the holy virgins on the right.

The antechambers to the Niche are decorated with murals, painted by Josep Obiols between 1945 and 1951. Firstly, we see angel musicians and emblems, and a Christ Pantocrator in the small apsidiole leading to the Niche; the second antechamber features portraits of Biblical women who prefigure Mary: Judith and Esther, Deborah and Ruth, whilst the frontal panel contains the names of the family which funded the work, and the Virgin, enthroned in the apsidiole. On the silver doors that provide access to the throne, made in 1956 and designed by Obiols, we see the Archangel Gabriel and Saint Joseph on entry and the evangelists John and Luke on leaving.

"La Moreneta", or Black Madonna, the sanctuary's centre, heart and raison d'être.

The central space, with the holy image, is entirely decorated by mosaics with a gilt background, made by Santiago Padrós (1918-1971), according to drawings produced by Josep Obiols. On the right-hand walls are three scenes concerning Mary "Mother of the Church", whilst on the left are another three alluding allude to Mary's status as the mother of Catalonia, monks and pilgrims.

The throne was designed by architect Folguera, in the style of a triptych whose centre is occupied by the holy image; on the sides we see the scenes of the Visitation and the Nativity of Mary, the two great festivities at Montserrat; the drawings were made by Josep Obiols. Over the cornice there is a semicircular arch with four silver angels holding Mary's royal emblems: the crown, the sceptre and a lily with three flowers.

The Chapel of the Niche

Planned and constructed between 1872 and 1887 by the architect Villar at first and completed by his son Villar i Carmona (1860-1927), the interior of this chapel is imbued with a truly special atmosphere created by the elliptical structure of the room and the profuse decoration, with abundant perforations and fretwork, in gilt and bright polychrome.

The charm of the room derives largely from the beautiful stained glass by Villar i Carmona, made by Antoni Rigalt in 1887. The beautiful mosaics in the small apse represent Jesus Crowning His Mother and were made by Santiago Padrós after drawings by Obiols. The sculpture of Saint George, which dates back to the year 1893, is by Agapit Vallmitjana.

Particularly outstanding is the mural painting in the dome, the work of the artist Joan Llimona. This painting is conceived as an apotheosis in which ecclesiastical and civil Catalonia pays homage to Our Lady of Montserrat. On the right are the holy pil-

The staircase up to the Shrine.

Vault and different views of the Shrine.

Partial view of the Shrine. >

grims, the last of whom is Bishop Torras i Bages. On the left are the shepherds who found the image, the kings of Aragon, the poets, the Council of One Hundred of Barcelona, a young married couple, boy choristers and, at the end, the donor. At the beginning and at the end are two symbolic figures: firstly, an angel of peace, arms outstretched and bearing olive branches; and, finally, Saint George slaying the dragon. The Madonna is in the centre of the dome, receiving the prayers of pilgrims who reach her heavenly throne at the hand of the angels. This painting, as beautiful as it is complex in its realisation, is one of the most outstanding works in Catalan modernist art.

The sacristy and partial views of the decoration on the vault, by the painter Josep Obiols.

The New Sacristy

This is the only space in the basilica described in this publication in which access is restricted due its private status. The New Sacristy was built by the architect Francesc Folguera and consists of a vestibule, a spacious room with wardrobes and a small apse. The ceiling, with barrel vault, was painted by Josep Obiols between 1943 and 1946. These mural paintings symbolise the liturgical year through the four seasons: winter, with the rising sun representing Christ; spring,

with the sacrificial lamb representing the Easter mystery; summer, with a radiant sun featuring the face of Christ; and autumn, with the Gospel roll and the throne of the Church awaiting Christ's return.

The mahogany wardrobes against the side walls are adorned by panels of marquetry, also designed by Obiols, representing saints and characters linked to Montserrat. The entire sacristy is most beautiful, with highly harmonious forms, demonstrating Obiols' *noucentista* ("19th-century") origins in all their splendour.

Different views of the Way.

Walks around the Sanctuary

The Degotalls Path

This route, which takes around 45 minutes to complete, begins before we reach Plaça dels Apòstols (Apostles Square); a sign here indicates "Els Degotalls - Camí del Magnificat" (Degotalls Parth - Way of the Magnificat). We encounter a sculpture of Monsignor Verdaguer, as we can see an important presence in the memory of Montserrat, at the start of a path devoted to artists. There follow other monuments, stelae and medallions commemorating famous people from our country: the writer Joan Maragall (1860-1911), the tenor Emili Vendrell (1893-1962), the composer Pep Ventura (1817-1875), the linguist Pompeu Fabra (1868-

Offerings to Our Lady. ›

1948), the musician Anselm Clave (1824-1874) and the master Lluis Millet (1867-1941).

Having completed this first section devoted to artists, we next come to some sixty beautiful majolicas representing the invocations that Catalan people have given to the Mother of God. At the end of this path, we come to a small square forming a cul-de-sac; to the left are Els Degotalls, a cave shelter blackened by damp due to the water that once filtered through its rocks, and which gives this path its name.

The Viewpoint of the Apostles.

The Viewpoint of the Apostles and Passeig de l'Escolania (Avenue of the Choir)

This is the first are that visitors coming to Montserrat by car or coach see on arrival. It owes its name to the Chapel of the Apostles, demolished in the early-20th century; in its place now stands a chapel-mausoleum devoted to the Requeté division, which fought in the Spanish Civil War (1936-1939).

At present, the area is dominated by the catering service building known as "El mirador dels Apòstols", built in 1976 under the aegis of Father Busquets (1925-2007), an architect and a monk at Montserrat. From the viewpoint in this building, the visitor commands magnificent views over the

Llobregat River Valley as the river passes through Monistrol at an altitude of 159 metres (we are at an altitude here of 720 metres). In the background are the Mediterranean Sea and Mount Tibidabo, rising over Barcelona; we can perfectly make out the silhouette of the telecommunications tower designed by Sir Norman Foster. Before us, to the left of the valley, is the Massif of Sant Llorenç del Munt with its peak, La Mola (1,102 meters), now part of Sant Llorenç del Munt i l'Obac Natural Park. At the end of this square and vantage point is a work by Josep Maria Subirachs (1927-2014), *The Stairway to Understanding*, a concrete monument standing 8.7 metres high and made in 1976. In it, the artist, then engaged in an abstract period in his work, alludes to the thought of the medieval philosopher Ramon Llull. The sculpture is formed by nine blocks that represent the different beings of creation, from the more material (stone) to the

most spiritual (God). Only the last of the steps, which are arranged in ascending order, is geometrically perfect, in the image of the Creator.

The avenue leading us to the next square is known as Passeig de l'Escolania, or Choir Walk. As the name suggests, we see, on our right, the building which houses the choristers during their years of study in Montserrat. The first monastic building we come to on the site, it is structured on four storeys: the first two floors contain the classrooms where the children study the general subjects, on the third are the music rooms and the top floor are the residential areas.

The next building we come to is the basilica, built in the 16th century and described in detail in the previous chapter of this book. From Passeig de l'Escolania we can observe the apse containing the Niche, adjoined to the rear of the building. This apse was altered between 1876 and 1878. The end of the basilica was flat until that time, when the architect Francisco de Paula del Villar Lozano (1828-1901) planned the three apses that we now see. Along the exterior of the building are stalls where mountain farmers sell their produce, which include, particularly, *mató* (milk curd) from around Marganell, and honey.

The last two buildings we encounter, parallel to each other along this avenue are the *mongia*, or monks' residence, and the abbot's tower. The first was built in the 18th century as part of an ambitious project to provide the monastery with spacious residential quarters. Austere, the building is well integrated into the side of the church, giving continuity to the monastery ensemble. The taller building is the tower that closes the monastery façade. The base of this contemporary structure is adorned by a relief, *Ariadne and Hermes*, also by the sculptor Josep Maria Subirachs.

The sight from the viewpoint.

The monastery ensemble is formed by two blocks of buildings with separate functions: on one side, we see the basilica and the monastery areas; on the other, the outbuildings, used to provide services for pilgrims and visitors.

Plaça de la Creu (Square of the Cross)

Since 2004, when the new rack railway line came into service, this square has regained its central importance, as it is the arrival point for visitors who use this means of transport. The current track from Monistrol de Montserrat follows the original route of the first rack railway, the oldest in Spain, which opened in 1892 and greatly improved access to the sanctuary on the part of the devout and pilgrims. The other means of public used to come up to the site is the characteristic yellow cable car, which entered into service in 1930 and has not changed colour since.

The name of the square alludes to the Cross of Saint Michael, a monumental work by Josep Maria Subirachs in 1962. The frontal part of this sculpture, modelled on the old wayside crosses, is engraved the name of the saint, patron of the mountain, and a symbol: the cross-sword that vanquishes the snake, and the meaning of the Archangel, which in Hebrew means "Who is like God?", written in different languages.

The Monumental Rosary

From this square, Plaça de la Creu, we take the Way of the Holy Cave (45 minutes). To the right of the long porch are some steps that lead us to the cable car station. We then continue along this delightful path whose construction, between 1693 and 1704, entailed overcoming many serious obstacles. In order to install the sculptures of the Mysteries of the Rosary, some of them markedly monumental, it was necessary to reorganise and adapt the path once more between 1898 and 1903. The inauguration of the Monumental Rosary in 1916 and the increasing number of visitors to the Holy Cave led to the construction of a funicular railway to link the sanctuary with the Way of the Holy Cave. We can take this line, which entered into service in 1929 and is still in operation today, in order to ascend the steepest section of the path without difficulty.

The Holy Cave.

First Glorious Mystery: The Resurrection of Christ, by the architect Antoni Gaudí (in cooperation with his assistant, Joan Rubió) and the sculptors Josep Llimona and Dionís Renart.

As for the construction of the Chapel of the Holy Cave, where, according to legend, shepherds found the image of the Our Lady of Montserrat, this dates back to the late-18th century and has been restored on several occasions since, always conserving its original Greek-cross structure domed roof and a Greek cross, domed cover and lantern. We can find other examples of Catalan baroque architecture in which sacred caves are integrated into buildings in the style of troglodyte chapels. The example nearest to Montserrat is the Cave of Saint Ignatius in Manresa, the city where the saint stopped to rest after his pilgrimage to Montserrat.

Stations of the Cross:

1. *First Joyful Mystery: The Annunciation.*
2. *Second Joyful Mystery: The Visitation of Mary to Elizabeth.*
3. *Third Joyful Mystery: The Nativity of Our Lord.*
4. *Fourth Joyful Mystery: The Presentation of Christ in the Temple.*
5. *Fifth Joyful Mystery: The Finding in the Temple.*
6. *First Sorrowful Mystery: Christ's Agony in the Garden of Gethsemane.*
7. *Second Sorrowful Mystery: The Scourging.*
8. *Third Sorrowful Mystery: The Crowning with Thorns.*
9. *Fourth Sorrowful Mystery: The Carrying of the Cross.*
10. *Fifth Sorrowful Mystery: The Crucifixion of Christ.*
11. *First Glorious Mystery: The Resurrection of Christ.*
12. *Second Glorious Mystery: The Ascension of Christ.*
13. *Third Glorious Mystery: The Descent of the Holy Spirit.*
14. *Fourth Glorious Mystery: The Assumption of Our Lady.*
15. *Fifth Glorious Mystery: The Coronation of Our Lady.*

Plaça Abat Oliba
(Abbot Oliba Square)

For many centuries, this square played a central role at the site, as the point of arrival for pilgrims reaching the sanctuary on foot along the Way of Saint Michael. Until quite recently, farmers used to sell their produce here, for which reason many still know it as "Plaça de les Pageses", or Farmers' Square. Today, the plaza is flanked lined by three buildings containing cells used as accommodation for visitors.

At the top of the steps, known as the "Staircase of the Poor" (the start of the route to Sant Jeroni through El Pla dels Ocells), stands a sculpture dedicated to the founding abbot, after whom the square is named. By Manuel Cusachs in 1992, this sculpture depicts the abbot seated on a chair, on the back of which are represented the belltowers of the monasteries of Ripoll and Sant Miquel de Cuixà, of which Oliba was abbot. In his left hand, he holds the plans for the old Romanesque Church of Montserrat, while with his right he makes a gesture of welcome to all who come to the monastery, according to the Benedictine tradition.

We leave the square through the gate in the old wall, emblazoned with the arms of Montserrat dating back to 1565, depicting the two characteristic features of Montserrat: the mountain and the saw. This shield also features also we can see the staff, indicating the status of the monastery as an abbey.

Plaça Abat Oliba: sculpture of the founding abbot.

The Way of the Cross

The path that leads to the Stations of the Cross begins in Plaça Abat Oliba, where we take the steps beside the fountain to reach the first station. The whole route takes about 20 minutes to complete. The Stations of the Cross is an act of devotion that reproduces the journey made by pilgrims to Jerusalem, along the *Via Dolorosa* or Way of Sorrows from the Palace of the Praetorian to the Holy Sepulchre. In this way, the faithful commemorate the Passion of Christ by visiting the main places on the path He took. This devout practice has spread throughout the Latin Church and is present in the main sanctuaries around world.

At Montserrat, a monumental Way of the Cross was built between 1904 and 1919, but the monuments along that first *Via Crucis* were destroyed during the Spanish Civil War, except for the Chapel of Sorrows, built by the architect Enric Sagnier

Chapel of Sorrow.

Station on the Way of the Cross.

(1858-1931) in 1916. This chapel stands at the end of the Way and houses the image of Our Lady of Sorrows, a sculpture by Jose Limon. A new Way of the Cross was designed in the 1950s by the architect Francesc Folquera (1891-1960).

The *Via Crucis* was divided into two clearly distinguished stages, the first featuring with sculptures by Margarita Sans Jordi (1911-2006) and Francesc Juventeny (1906-1990), whilst works by Domènec Fita (1927) adorn the second part.

Stations on the Way of the Cross.

The squares of Saint Mary

In the first level of the squares we find a statue of Saint George, patron saint of Catalonia, carved in travertine stone by Josep Maria Subirachs in 1986. As we can see, this sculptor's works are very much present in the public spaces of the sanctuary. This piece belongs to the new stage in Subirachs' artistic development, in which he uses the negative form to create surprising optical effects that enable us to appreciate the figuration without entering the realm of realism.

Near to the rocks of the mountain stands the Hostal Abat Cisneros. The dining room in this hostel is housed in the old monastery stables, a spectacular building whose ceiling is formed by a stone vault and whose walls are the very stone of the mountain. The year 1563, which is emblazoned on the facade of the hostel, attests to the historic value of this building. Before the door stands a wayside cross indicating the end of a path. It is a copy of the 16th-century original. We can see one of the two original wayside crosses conserved in the Audiovisual Space "Inside Montserrat".

From these squares, we can observe the monastery façade, made from polished stone quarried in the mountain. The façade was designed by the Francesc Folguera (1861-1960) and built between 1942 and 1968. At the top we can read the Latin inscription *Urbs Jerusalem Beata Dicta Pacis Vi-*

Main façade.

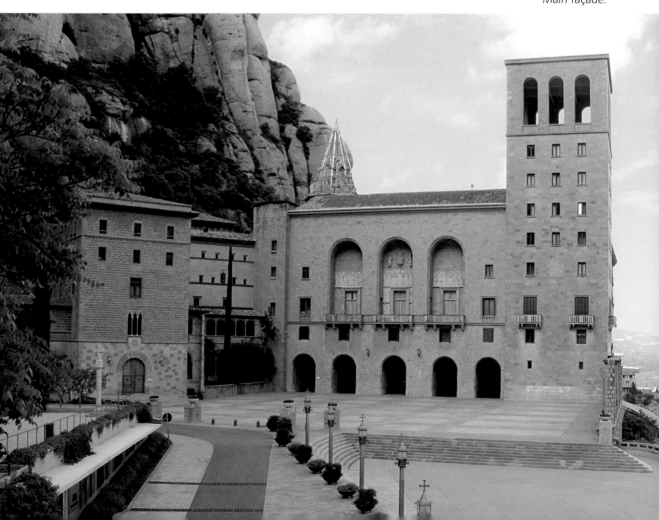

Montserrat.

sio ("Blessed city of Jerusalem, called "Vision of Peace"). The sculptures on the façade are by the sculptor Joan Rebull (1899-1981). The frieze on the left depicts the «Transit of Saint Benedict», evoking the saint›s death. The central frieze is more complex, as a whole evoking the proclamation of the dogma of the Assumption of Mary. This ensemble features the huge figure of Mary elevated to Heaven in an attitude of prayer, flanked by two angel monks. In the third frieze, we see Saint George with a representation of the monks who died during the Spanish Civil War (1936-1939).

Gothic cloister.

Gothic cloister: corridor on the ground floor.

To the left of the facade we can see half of the monastery's Gothic cloister, the finest architectural and sculptural heritage conserved at Montserrat from the Gothic period. The cloister was built during the abbacy of Giuliano della Rovere, an outstanding figure who became Pope in 1503, adopting the name of Julius II; although he never visited Montserrat, ruling the monastery from a distance and through administrators, he was an excellent abbot, proposed by Rome during a period when government was difficult due to the tumultuous events that were taking place at the time. The cloister is a fine work of Late Catalan Gothic, with slender columns and capitals adorned by floral motifs, as well as heads of men and women with the bodies of fantastic, often winged, animals, and other fabulous beasts that blend in with the floral decoration and the hooded heads of monks with

the bodies of beasts and the wings of bats. Some of the brackets are also adorned by the emblems of Montserrat and Cardinal della Rovere, this a simple oak tree. The cloister also has a second storey above, this adorned by more simple capitals.

Under the arches of the facade lie the tombs of John of Aragon and Bernat de Vilamarí, both dating back to the 16th century. John of Aragon, Duke of Luna and Count of Ribagorça, was the grandson of King Ferdinand the Catholic; in 1508, whilst he was viceroy of Naples, he order the construction of this tomb, in which he is portrayed as young and at prayer, looking towards Our Lady of Montserrat. Bernat de Vilamarí died in Naples in 1516, and his wife and daughter commissioned the construction of his funeral monument, which takes the form of a triumphal arch, its central section occupied by the sarcophagus with recumbent image of this admiral.

The tombs of Bernat de Vilamarí and John of Aragon.

Museum of Montserrat: interior views.

The Museum of Montserrat

The building

The Museum of Montserrat occupies the entire area beneath the three squares that stand before the monastery, which were also built by the architect Josep Puig i Cadafalch as part of an integral project for the architectural and urban reform Montserrat, carried out between 1929 and 1933.

The first thing the visitor sees is the large vestibule housing the gift shop and ticket offices. This vestibule, which is structured by pillars that divide the space into twelve sections covered by Catalan vaults, was originally used for washing and drying, as well as serving as a residence for staff employed at the sanctuary. The building that houses the permanent exhibition in the museum is also interesting due to its architectural quality and unusual structure. The upper floor of the museum is supported by steel parabolic arches that rest on the rock and on the façade that compensates for the difference in level between the squares. The lower

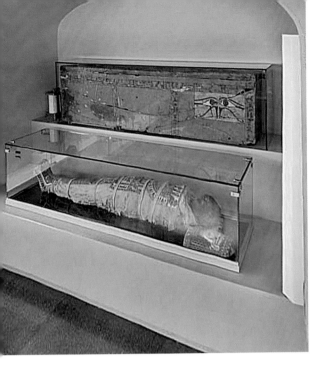

floor is sustained by these beams, supported by slender steel girders, thus freeing this level from pillars and impediments of all kinds.

The archaeological collection

The objects displayed in the archaeological section of the museum were brought here, in the main, from the old Biblical Museum, which opened in 1911 under the aegis of Father Bonaventura Ubach (1879-1960), who undertook many great journeys of exploration to search for data to help to understand and spread our understanding of the Bible based on the cultural context in which it was written. In 1962, this museum was reorganised according to strictly archaeological criteria and now contains the following sections: Middle East, Egypt, Cyprus, Italy and the Hellenic World, Early Roman Empire and Early Christian Culture. The outstanding objects here include the collection of cuneiform tablets, one of the most important worldwide, and the Egyptian funeral goods, which illustrate life, customs, culture and religion in the Egypt of the Pharaohs.

The painting collections

The Museum of Montserrat also houses one of the most important collections of paintings in Catalonia. The first room is devoted to ancient painting (13th-18th centuries), particularly Italian works. As in the case of the Library, Abbot Marcet also played a major role here, purchasing these paintings in Rome and Naples between 1911 and 1920 The most outstanding include Caravaggio's *Penitent Saint Jerome* and Gianbattista Tiepolo's *Allegory on the Birth of Francis I of Austria*. This section also features works from the history of Spanish painting by such artists as Pedro Berruguete and El Greco.

The period most fully represented is Catalan painting from the 19th and 20th centuries. The first great masterpiece from this period is Marià Fortuny's *The Tapestry Merchant*, the starting point for a journey that takes us through the realism of

Ramon Martí Alsina and the landscapes of the Olot School, featuring works by Joaquim Vayreda, to modernism. This flourishing period in the history of Catalan art is superbly represented in the museum with works by such artists as Ramon Casas, Santiago Rusiñol, Joaquim Mir Isidre Nonell and Hermen Anglada Camarassa, among many others. This collection of Catalan art is complemented by a selection of works by contemporary painters such as Darío de Regoyos, Joaquim Sorolla and Ignacio de Zuloaga, and two paintings, *The Old Fisherman* and *Altar Boy*, by a young Pablo Picasso. The vast majority of these paintings were donated by Josep Sala Ardiz in 1982.

The visitor will also find a small collection of paintings by great masters of French Impressionism, which includes works by Claude Monet, Alfred Sisley, Camille Pissarro, Auguste Renoir and Edgar Degas, thanks to a donation made by the architect Xavier Busquets in 1990. The painting collection is completed by a growing selection of avant-garde art, most notably Salvador Dalí's work *Neo-Cubist Academy*, the abstraction of Serge Poliakoff, works by internationally-known artists like Joaquim Torres Garcia, George Rouault and Jean Metzinger, and avant-garde Catalan art since the 1970s, including pieces by Antoni Tàpies, Ràfols Casamada and Josep Maria Subirachs, amongst others. Some of these works were donated to the museum by the artists themselves, a fact that reflects the institution's commitment to contemporary art, which is showcased particularly in the temporary exhibitions. Finally, we should mention the Irish-born painter Sean Scully's donation in 2010 of his work *Oisin's Mountain*.

< *The Penitent Saint Jerome, produced by Caravaggio (1571-1610) in around 1605, fully illustrates the innovations of an artist considered the first painter of the Modern Age: a new, naturalist sensitivity and a vision based on chiaroscuro.*

Ramon Martí Alsina (Barcelona, 1826 – 1894) Portrait of the artist Ramon Tusquets.

Joaquim Vayreda (Girona, 1843 – Olot, 1894): Young Peasant.

‹ *Ramon Casas (1866-1932) is the modernist painter whose work is imbued with the greatest power and expressive intensity, especially when taking the female figure as its theme. The Museum of Montserrat collection includes more than twenty oil paintings by this artist, which combines with works by other great masters of Catalan modernism to form an outstanding selection of this artistic movement, known internationally as Art Nouveau, the most important at around the turn of the 20th century.*

Romà Ribera: Exit from the Dance *(1913).*

Isidre Nonell: Consuelo *(1901).*

Joaquim Mir: The Way of the Cave *(1908).*

Joaquim Torres Garcia: New York *(1929).*

Josep Llimona: Regina Sacratissimi Rossarii.

Edgar Degas: Unhappy Nelly *(1834 – 1917)*.

Francesc Torrescassana: Girl before the Piano *(1885)*.

Museum: the "Nigra sum" exhibition room.

Other collections in the Museum

The "Nigra Sum" section includes a varied sample of artistic and popular objects illustrating the iconographic evolution over the centuries of the holy image and the way it is rendered in very different works. The visitor can admire a large and interesting collection of pieces from the baroque and modernist periods to contemporary art; for modern artists have also taken inspiration from the most iconic religious image pertaining to the Catalan people.

The exhibition devoted to the Eastern Church, "Phos Hilaron" ("Hail Gladdening Light"), illustrates, through holy icons surrounded by the golden light of Byzantine churches, the faces and the mysteries and the glory of Jesus Christ, Our Lady, the saints and the feasts on the liturgical calendar.

Our Lady of Montserrat, by Josep Maria Subirachs. (2001).

Our Lady of Montserrat, by Josep Maria Subirachs. (2001).

Finally, religious precious gold- and silver-work constituted the most important artistic heritage at monastery and the sanctuary of Montserrat during the years preceding the above-described events of the early-19th century, the French War and disentailment. Unfortunately, most of this great treasure was lost. However, since the restoration of the monastery, a new collection of such pieces of the highest material and artistic value from the 19th and 20th centuries has been built up. A small sample of works from this important collection are on show in the Museum.

Our Lady of Montserrat,
by Joaquim Vayreda.
(1884).

Precious metalwork.

ACUE

29 JUNY DE 1912

ROMERÍA
DELS NOYS DE CATALUNYA
Á MONTSERRAT

VIROLAI

Rosa d'abril, Morena de la serra,
de Montserrat Estel,
il·lumineu la catalana terra,
guieu-nos cap al cel.

Amb serra d'or els angelets serraren
eixos turons per fer-vos un palau;
Reina del Cel que els Serafins baixaren
deu-nos abric dins vostre mantell blau.

Alba naixent d'estrelles coronada,
Ciutat de Déu que somnià David,
a vostres peus la lluna s'és posada,
el sol sos raigs us dóna per vestit.

Dels catalans sempre sereu Princesa,
dels espanyols l'Estrella d'Orient,
sigueu pels bons pilar de fortalesa,
pels pecadors el port de salvament.

Doneu consol a qui la pàtria enyora
sens veure mai els cims de Montserrat;
en terra i mar oïu a qui us implora,
torneu a Déu els cors que l'han deixat.

Mística Font de l'aigua de la vida,
rageu del Cel al cor de mon país,
dons i virtuts deixeu-li per florida; feu-ne,
si us plau, el vostre paradís.

Ditxosos ulls, Maria, els que us vegen,
ditxós el cor que s'obre a vostra llum;
Rosa del Cel que els Serafins voltegen,
a ma oració doneu vostre perfum.

Cedre gentil del Líbano corona,
Arbre d'encens, Palmera de Sion,
el fruit sagrat que vostre amor ens dóna,
és Jesucrist, el Redemptor del món.

Amb vostre nom comença nostra història,
i és Montserrat el nostre Sinaí;
siguin per tots l'escala de la glòria
eixos penyals coberts de romaní.

JACINT VERDAGUER

Contents